MEGAWORDS 4
Multisyllabic Words for Reading, Spelling, and Vocabulary

KRISTIN JOHNSON   POLLY BAYRD

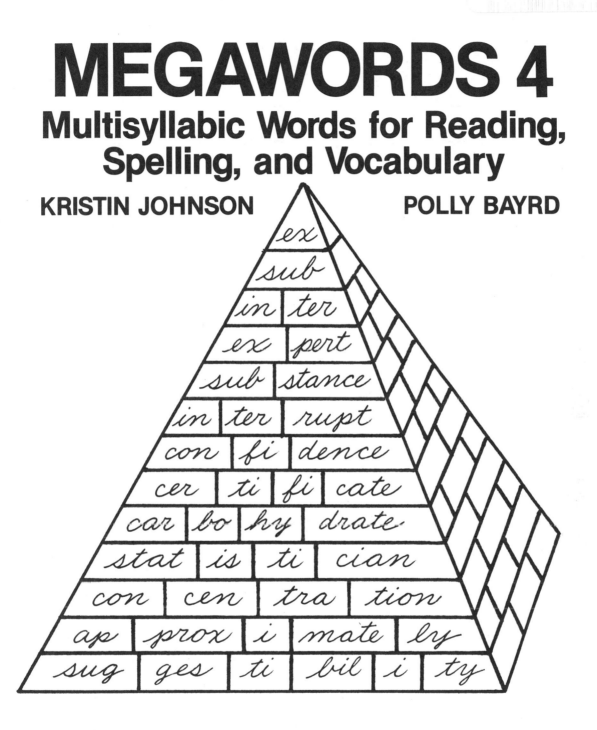

Educators Publishing Service, Inc.
Cambridge and Toronto

eps

Educators Publishing Service, Inc.
31 Smith Place, Cambridge, Massachusetts 02138-1000

May 1994 Printing

Contents

TO THE STUDENT

Megawords 4: Multisyllabic Words for Reading, Spelling, and Vocabulary is the fourth in a series of books designed to help you read and spell words that contain two or more syllables. The words are organized into lists according to their phonetic structure. Worksheets following each list explain and help you practice the rules or patterns found in that particular group of words. Some exercises focus on reading the words; others focus on spelling or vocabulary.

Megawords is designed to meet your individual learning needs. You and your teacher can decide which lists you need to study (and which you already know) by interpreting your results on the Check Test. You may need to focus on reading *and* spelling. Or you may need to use *Megawords* only to improve spelling skills. You and your teacher can record your progress on the Accuracy Checklist at the back of your book.

We think that it is important for you to be able to 1) sound out words and 2) learn to read them proficiently and fluently. You and your teacher will set a reading rate goal. When you can read the words easily and automatically, you will be less likely to forget the words and you can concentrate on reading for meaning instead of on sounding out words. You can keep track of your reading rate on the Proficiency Graph at the end of your book.

Megawords 4 focuses on suffixes and endings such as *-tion, -ture, -ous,* and *-ible*. Often these suffixes and endings are not spelled the way they sound or pronounced the way they look. However, once you learn their pronunciations and spellings, you will be able to read and spell quite long and complex words. *Megawords 4* also shows you the typical accent patterns found in these words.

We hope that you will be interested in checking out your skills in reading and spelling multisyllabic words—in seeing what you know and what you need to learn. In addition, we hope that you will enjoy tackling new word groups and mastering them. We think that multisyllabic words, when presented clearly and in patterned groups, can be challenging and fun. We sincerely hope that you enjoy and experience success with *Megawords*.

Polly Bayrd
Kristin Johnson

LIST 20: *-er, -or, -ar, -ard,* AND *-ward*

-er	*-or*	*-or*	*-ar*	*-ard,* *-ward*
* teacher	* humor	* professor	* dollar	* standard
* power	* honor	* translator	collar	blizzard
writer	* color	* visitor	cellar	buzzard
* father	* labor	educator	pillar	* mustard
barber	* favor	elevator	* regular	custard
destroyer	tumor	* operator	* popular	hazard
islander	error	inventor	* similar	wizard
character	vapor	assessor	singular	lizard
* remember	* actor	splendor	* circular	haggard
announcer	vigor	instructor	particular	drunkard
welder	* major	inspector	muscular	scabbard
* sister	minor	radiator	scholar	leopard
roster	terror	calculator	perpendicular	orchard
murder	pastor	* refrigerator	solar	Richard
golfer	editor	legislator	* sugar	Leonard
banker	* tractor	dictator	liar	Howard
printer	* doctor	* scissors	vinegar	steward
fluster			* grammar	coward
butler			beggar	upward
* lumber			nectar	* forward
plaster			bursar	* afterward
stutter			cedar	westward
wander			* calendar	inward
hamster			vulgar	onward
filter			Oscar	* toward
yonder				homeward
chapter				awkward

* Practical spelling words. The teacher and student should decide together how many of these words the student will be responsible for spelling.

-er, -or, and *-ar* are endings that say /ər/.
-ard is an ending that says /ərd/.
-ward is an ending that says /wərd/.

Pronounce and combine the syllables. Then cover the divided word and practice reading the whole word. Circle the ending as shown.

bar ber	barber
mo tor	motor
cel lar	cellar
ce dar	cedar
li ar	liar
doc tor	doctor
sis ter	sister
fa vor	favor
wri ter	writer
ma jor	major

re mem ber	remember
vis i tor	visitor
pop u lar	popular
vin e gar	vinegar
an nounc er	announcer
jan i tor	janitor
reg u lar	regular
cal en dar	calendar
de stroy er	destroyer
in ven tor	inventor

op er a tor	operator
ra di a tor	radiator
el e va tor	elevator
cal cu la tor	calculator
par tic u lar	particular

stan dard	standard
mus tard	mustard
haz ard	hazard
wiz ard	wizard
drunk ard	drunkard

on ward	onward
up ward	upward
west ward	westward
for ward	forward

WORKSHEET 20–B

Match the syllables to make real words. Say each word aloud as you write it.

bar	tor	_____		li	ber	_____
doc	dard	_____		lum	gar	_____
stan	ber	_barber_		vul	ar	_____

so	zard	_____		cow	lar	_____
trac	lar	_____		col	er	_____
bliz	tor	_____		pow	ard	_____

ac	vor	_____		mi	chard	_____
fa	tor	_____		for	nor	_____
cus	tard	_____		or	ward	_____

Unscramble these three-syllable words.

mem re ber _____   in tor struc _____

u lar pop _____   dar cal en _____

Bonus words:

cu tor la cal _____

tor op a er _____

di a ra tor _____

frig a re er tor _____

What letter comes just before *or* in the bonus words above? _____

Review: Three ways to spell the ending /ər/ are _____, _____, and _____.

WORKSHEET 20–C

Three ways to spell the ending /ər/ are *er, or,* and *ar.* Sometimes it is hard to tell how to spell the /ər/ sound. Here are three helpful hints:

    er is used most of the time. When in doubt, use *er.*

    or is often used after *t.*

    ar is often used after *l.*

You will spell all the words on this worksheet correctly if you follow the three hints above. Fill in the correct ending. Then copy the word.

teach____	_____	act____	_____
visit____	_____	barb____	_____
rememb____	_____	cell____	_____
doct____	_____	weld____	_____
lumb____	_____	popul____	_____
murd____	_____	elevat____	_____
regul____	_____	pow____	_____
schol____	_____	simil____	_____
moth____	_____	memb____	_____
educat____	_____	operat____	_____
bank____	_____	fath____	_____
sol____	_____	doll____	_____
hamm____	_____	circul____	_____
golf____	_____	wond____	_____
credit____	_____	edit____	_____
muscul____	_____	summ____	_____
yond____	_____	particul____	_____
translat____	_____	pill____	_____
temp____	_____	off____	_____
mot____	_____	refrigerat____	_____

WORKSHEET 20-D

Your teacher will dictate some words. Sound out each word as you write the missing syllable(s). Then write the whole word, saying it aloud as you spell it.

	Copy	ABC Order
1. _____ er	_____	_____
2. doc _____	_____	_____
3. _____ lar	_____	_____
4. bar _____	_____	_____
5. mo _____	_____	_____
6. mus _____	_____	_____
7. stan _____	_____	_____
8. awk _____	_____	_____
9. _____ mem _____	_____	_____
10. pop _____ _____	_____	_____
11. in _____ tor	_____	_____
12. _____ _____ dar	_____	_____

Bonus:

13. _____ _____ _____ _____ lar	_____	

In these words, the middle consonant has to be doubled to make the vowel in the first syllable short. Read the clue to figure out the word. Fill in the doubled consonant and then write the word.

The part of a shirt or dress around the neck	co __ __ ar	_____
The study of nouns and verbs, etc.	gra __ __ ar	_____
A bad snowstorm with wind	bli __ __ ard	_____
A person who begs for money	be __ __ ar	_____
Four quarters, ten dimes, twenty nickels, or one hundred pennies	do __ __ ar	_____

Now go back and write the words at the top of the page in alphabetical order.

WORKSHEET 20–E

-er, *-or*, *-ar*, and *-ward* are unaccented endings. The accent falls on another syllable in the word. The dark lines and accent marks in this book are *accent patterns* (__ ´ __). Each line stands for one syllable. The accent mark shows which syllable is accented.[1]

Review these accent patterns:

__ ´ __   Accent on the first syllable
The accent is usually on the first syllable in two-syllable words *(stan´ dard, sis´ ter, dol´ lar).*

__ ´ __ __   Accent on the first syllable
The accent is usually on the first syllable in three-syllable words *(vis´ i tor, char´ ac ter).*

__ __ ´ __   Accent on the second syllable
The accent is usually on the second syllable in three-syllable words that contain a prefix, root, and suffix *(de stroy´ er, in ven´ tor).*

Write these words by syllables, noting the accent patterns. Write the accented syllables in the boxes.

Accent the First Syllable		Accent the Second Syllable	
motor	⬚ ____	announcer	____ ⬚ ____
scissors	⬚ ____	remember	____ ⬚ ____
liar	⬚ ____	inspector	____ ⬚ ____
visitor	⬚ ____ ____	professor	____ ⬚ ____
calendar	⬚ ____ ____	instructor	____ ⬚ ____
vinegar	⬚ ____ ____	inventor	____ ⬚ ____
similar	⬚ ____ ____	destroyer	____ ⬚ ____
circular	⬚ ____ ____		
popular	⬚ ____ ____		

[1] A Summary of Accent Patterns is on pages 77 and 78.

WORKSHEET 20–F

Write each word in the correct set of boxes by paying attention to the ending and the number of syllables in the word.

particular	catcher	afterward	elevator	similar	backward
standard	power	operator	custard	remember	mustard
favor	contractor	calendar	sugar	perpendicular	character

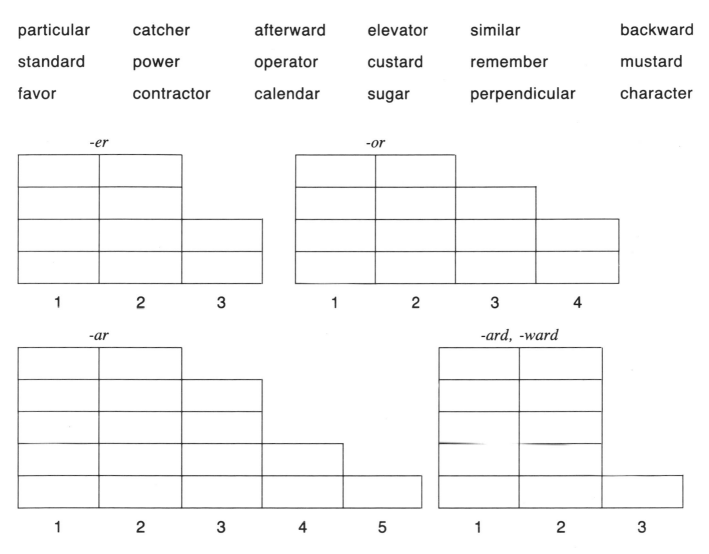

Proofing Practice: Three common List 20 words are misspelled in each of the sentences below. Correct them as shown.

Leonard
1. ~~Leonerd~~ was quite flustered when he found the hamstor behind the refrigeratar.

2. The inspecter who checked the elevatar called a weldor to repair it.

3. Too much suger spoiled the custerd that our instructer made.

WORKSHEET 20–G

Circle the /ər/ sound in each of these words. Then write each word under the appropriate heading.

* circul(ar)	inventor	* grammar	* remember
* visitor	radiator	character	cedar
* scissors	anchor	professor	* father
islander	* tractor	editor	* farmer
* dollar	announcer	labor	* calendar
* cellar	* sugar	splendor	* popular
* similar	* teacher	* regular	* refrigerator

-er	-or	-ar
_____	_____	_circular_
_____	_____	_____
_____	_____	_____
_____	_____	_____
_____	_____	_____
_____	_____	_____
_____	_____	_____
_____	_____	_____
	_____	

Review: _er_, _ar_, and _or_ are three ways to spell the ending ⌊_____⌋ .

Have another student test you on spelling the starred words. They are practical spelling words.

My score: _____ words correct.

WORKSHEET 20–H

Add *or* to verbs that end in *ate* to make nouns. Remember to drop the final *e* because you are adding an ending that begins with a vowel.

Verb	Noun	Verb	Noun
refrigerate	*refrigerator*	illustrate	_____
educate	_____	radiate	_____
dictate	_____	operate	_____
translate	_____	investigate	_____
calculate	_____		

Add the suffix *-or* to these verbs to change them to nouns.

Verb	Noun	Verb	Noun
act	*actor*	invent	_____
instruct	_____	assess	_____
visit	_____	conduct	_____

Use *or* at the end of the incomplete words below. Write the ten *or* words at the bottom of the page.

A good friend did me a fav _____ by taking me on a maj _____ tour of New England. With vim and vig _____, we set out to see the splend _____ of the mountains. We had some min _____ problems with our car, but with a bit of lab _____ and few err _____ s, we got it fixed. We arrived in time to see the glam _____ ous col _____ of the maple leaves. We were in quite good hum _____!

_____ _____ _____ _____

_____ _____ _____ _____

_____   _____

9

WORKSHEET 20-I

In each group of three words, circle the spelling that looks right to you. Then check your answers with the words on the bottom of the page. Write the correct spelling on the line. All of these words are practical spelling words. Study them and have another student test you on them.

favor
faver   _____
favar

charactar
charactor   _____
character

doller
dollor   _____
dollar

calendor
calendar   _____
calender

similar
similor   _____
similer

power
powar   _____
powor

grammer
grammar   _____
grammor

labor
laber   _____
labar

sugor
suger   _____
sugar

humer
humor   _____
humar

auther
author   _____
authar

scissors
scissers   _____
scissars

Answers:
favor, dollar, similar, grammar, sugar, author, character, calendar, power, labor, humor, scissors.

My spelling score: _____ words correct.

10

WORKSHEET 20–J

Some words that end in *or* are abstract nouns. They are names of things you cannot touch, feel, or see. Fill in the blanks with the correct abstract nouns.

color	major	terror	favor	honor
labor	humor	valor	minor	flavor

1. While you are up, please do me a _____ and get my fountain pen.

2. Heather has a terrific sense of _____; she is very funny.

3. Roger was filled with _____ after seeing the scary movie.

4. The knight displayed his _____ by defeating the villain.

5. The spices add _____ to the vegetables.

6. What _____ scarf are you looking for?

7. Wilbur's _____ in college was English; his _____ was art.

8. On my _____, I will try to do my best.

9. The _____ charges for rebuilding the engine were more than the parts.

Sometimes words that end in *or* are lengthened by the addition of other suffixes or endings. Underline the letters *or* in these longer words; then write the root. When you have finished, start at the arrow, and use the clues to fit the longer words into the puzzle.

vig**or**ous   *vigor*

colorful _____

humorous _____

favorite _____

flavorful _____

minority _____

majority _____

glamorous _____

honorable _____

favorable _____

11

WORKSHEET 20-K

Complete each sentence with an *-ard* or *-ward* word from below that makes sense.

blizzard	buzzard	awkward	leopard	homeward
cowards	toward	orchard	Edward	backward
forward		onward		Richard

1. Esther fell over _ _ _ _ _ _ _ _ on her bike.

2. Walter was quite _ _ _ _ _ _ _ on the new skates.

3. Eleanor ran _ _ _ _ _ _ the frightened child.

4. After the _ _ _ _ _ _ _ killed and ate most of the zebra, the

_ _ _ _ _ _ _ ate the rest.

As _ _ _ _ _ _ and _ _ _ _ _ _ _ walked _ _ _ _ _ _ _ _ _,

they passed the old apple _ _ _ _ _ _ _. The trees were bare now and covered

with snow from the last _ _ _ _ _ _ _ _. It was late at night and dark as they

trudged _ _ _ _ _ _ through the deep snow. They felt like _ _ _ _ _ _ _,

but they couldn't help it. They were afraid and looked _ _ _ _ _ _ _ _ to their

warm, bright room at home.

Some *-or* words are nouns that name a person who has a certain job.
Fill in each blank with the correct noun. The italicized word is your clue.

1. An _educator_ works to *educate* children.

2. An _____ *illustrates* and an _____ *edits* books.

3. A P.I., or private _____, *investigates* crimes.

4. There are one hundred _____ in the *senate*.

5. Many _____ worked for years to *translate* the Bible.

6. The telephone _____ *operates* the switchboard.

7. Which _____ will win the award for best *acting*?

8. The building _____ discovered a leaky pipe during the *inspection*.

12

WORKSHEET 20-L

Twenty different words end with -*ard* or -*ward* in this story. Circle the words and write them on the lines provided below. Some of the words may have other endings after *ard* or *ward* (for example, *backwards*). Write each word once.

(Leonard) the lizard and Howard the wizard lived in an orchard behind a castle. Leonard was your standard lizard, able to crawl both backwards and forwards. Howard, however, was more than a wizard; he was also a drunkard. The steward of the castle gave him large tankards of wine. Afterwards, when he was drunk, he was such a coward that he thought it would be hazardous to pull his sword out of its scabbard. He tried to hide the odor of wine by eating mustard and custard, but the lizard could always tell Howard was drunk by his haggard look. They lived in the orchard until Howard got lost in a blizzard and Leonard decided to move westward.

<table>
<tr><td colspan="2" align="center">-ard</td><td align="center">-ward</td></tr>
<tr><td>Leonard</td><td></td><td></td></tr>
<tr><td></td><td></td><td></td></tr>
<tr><td></td><td></td><td></td></tr>
<tr><td></td><td></td><td></td></tr>
<tr><td></td><td></td><td></td></tr>
<tr><td></td><td></td><td></td></tr>
<tr><td></td><td></td><td></td></tr>
</table>

Write the correct word from above next to its definition.

1. A case to put a sword in   _____

2. A tall drinking cup with a handle   _____

3. A person who manages a big kitchen   _____

4. A place where fruit trees grow   _____

5. Careworn; wild-looking from pain or worry _____

WORKSHEET 20—M

Read the following sentences and circle all the List 20 words that you can find.

1. The inventor showed the welder how to make a motor for the new tractor.
2. Golfers and fishers may be liars, but pastors don't wander from the truth.
3. The burglar went into the cellar and rode the elevator past the sleeping janitor.
4. The contractor won an award for that cedar house with the solar heating system.
5. Do you remember who the author of that popular book is?
6. Oscar put the custard, which was made with eggs and sugar, in the refrigerator.
7. Would you rather be a teacher, doctor, janitor, or steward?
8. My sister Jennifer has a rotten sense of humor.
9. Eleanor hates the flavor of vinegar.
10. The muscular visitor fell backwards in the blizzard.
11. That announcer is quite a colorful character.

Look at List 20. Choose five words and write them in sentences below.

_____

_____

_____

_____

_____

Take out a piece of blank paper. Your teacher will dictate three of the sentences above for you to write.

You have completed the worksheets for List 20. Now it is time to check your accuracy in reading and spelling. Read and spell ten words selected by your teacher, and record your scores on the Accuracy Checklist. Work toward 90–100 percent accuracy.

When you have achieved 90–100 percent accuracy in reading, build up your reading speed. Decide on your rate goal with your teacher. Record your rate on the Proficiency Graph.

My goal for reading List 20 is _____ words per minute with two or fewer errors.

14

LIST 21: *-tion*

Two Syllables	Three Syllables	Three Syllables	Three Syllables	Four Syllables
* station	* addition	* correction	* adoption	* conversation
* action	commotion	* attraction	* donation	* transportation
caption	* completion	extortion	* deduction	* information
* notion	* ambition	* collection	* emotion	conservation
* fiction	* pollution	* direction	* relation	* observation
portion	starvation	assertion	* solution	* concentration
function	* condition	inscription	tradition	exportation
diction	* dictation	injection	devotion	* education
junction	carnation	conviction	* election	* explanation
* caution	ignition	* inspection	quotation	* expectation
faction	temptation	addiction	munition	dissertation
lotion	partition	* corruption	* location	interruption
option	cognition	consumption	promotion	* illustration
* motion	sensation	* subscription	rejection	constellation
* fraction	* inflation	* subtraction	probation	confirmation
auction	formation	contraption	* edition	compensation
* nation	contrition	distinction	* position	condemnation
* section	ablution	* construction	vocation	* operation
ration	foundation	* infection	petition	consultation
* mention	* creation	* objection	eruption	contemplation
	salvation	disruption	oration	condensation
	plantation	* perfection	projection	
	* taxation	connection	presumption	Five Syllables
	translation	* attention	* nutrition	* examination
	damnation	* invention	* prescription	* investigation
	* frustration			* congratulations
				* administration

* Practical spelling words. The teacher and student should decide together how many of these words the student will be responsible for spelling.

15

WORKSHEET 21–A

-tion is a common ending in many multisyllabic words. *-tion* nearly always says /shən/. The syllable just before *-tion* is accented. Vowels that come just before *-tion* are long, except for *i*, which is always short (/ĭ/).

Pronounce and combine the syllables to read the whole word. Draw a box around the accented syllable, and mark the long and short accented vowels.

    — ´ —

lo tion	lotion
cau tion	caution
junc tion	junction

    — ´ —

por tion	portion
frac tion	fraction
auc tion	auction

    — — ´ —

am bi tion	ambition
com mo tion	commotion
so lu tion	solution
ig ni tion	ignition
e lec tion	election
tra di tion	tradition

    — — ´ —

quo ta tion	quotation
star va tion	starvation
com ple tion	completion
pre sump tion	presumption
dis tinc tion	distinction
nu tri tion	nutrition

    — — — ´ —

op er a tion	operation
con cen tra tion	concentration
in ter rup tion	interruption
ex pec ta tion	expectation

    — — — — ´ —

ad min is tra tion	administration
in ves ti ga tion	investigation

Unscramble these three-syllable words.

tion fla in	_____	di tion rec	_____
lu so tion	_____	trac tion at	_____
lu pol tion	_____	tion rup e	_____
tri nu tion	_____	scrip sub tion	_____
tion car na	_____	tion ob jec	_____
rup tion cor	_____	am tion bi	_____
tion a cre	_____	tion frus tra	_____
e tion mo	_____	si po tion	_____

Unscramble these four- and five-syllable words.

sa con tion ver _____

ter in tion rup _____

por tion trans ta _____

am na tion i ex _____

ti tion in ga ves _____

In the following words, *tion* may sound more like /chən/ than /shən/. Pronounce and combine the syllables to read the whole word. Draw a box around the accented syllable and mark the long and short accented vowels.

men tion	mention
at ten tion	attention
in ven tion	invention

Review: The accent always falls on the syllable just _____ -tion. Vowels that come

before -tion are _____, except for *i,* which is always _____.

WORKSHEET 21–C

Your teacher will dictate some words. Sound out each word as you write the missing syllable(s). Then write the whole word, saying it aloud as you spell it.

	Copy	ABC Order
1. _____ tion	_____	_____
2. mo _____	_____	_____
3. car _____ tion	_____	_____
4. _____ tra tion	_____	_____
5. in _____ tion	_____	_____
6. _____ ta tion	_____	_____
7. _____ a tion	_____	_____
8. in _____ tion	_____	_____
9. tra _____ tion	_____	_____
10. ob _____ va tion	_____	_____
11. _____ ter _____ tion	_____	_____
12. pre _____ tion	_____	_____
13. il lus _____ _____	_____	_____
14. sub _____ _____	_____	_____
15. _____ _____ tion	_____	_____

Now go back and write the words in alphabetical order.

Choose three words from above and write them in sentences.

_____

_____

_____

_____

_____

WORKSHEET 21-D

In the following words, first count and underline the sounded vowels. The number of sounded vowels tells you the number of syllables in the word. Then circle the common prefixes and word endings. Finally, apply the syllabication rules to the middle of the words, and mark the vowel sounds. The first one is done for you.

	Number of Syllables		Number of Syllables		Number of Syllables
(con)sulta(tion)	4	probation	_____	examination	_____
observation	_____	prescription	_____	disruption	_____
administration	_____	deduction	_____	investigation	_____
dissertation	_____	constellation	_____	expectation	_____
objection	_____	perfection	_____	subscription	_____
congratulations	_____	translation	_____	confirmation	_____
adoption	_____	inspection	_____	promotion	_____
conviction	_____	contemplation	_____	explanation	_____
confirmation	_____	addiction	_____	information	_____

Review: A prefix is a word part that comes _____ a root.

Find twelve common prefixes in the words above and list them below.

_____	_____	_____	_____
_____	_____	_____	_____
_____	_____	_____	_____

WORKSHEET 21–E

Review: The syllable j_____ b_____ the ending -*tion* is accented. Vowels that come just before -*tion* are _____, except for *i*, which is _____ (/ĭ/).

Divide the following words into syllables. Then copy them syllable-by-syllable into the boxes below. Mark the long and short vowels in the accented syllables as shown.

emotion	station	exportation	salvation	concentration
transportation	creation	position	nutrition	administration
ignition	ambition	munition	expectation	auction
examination		confirmation		interruption

Two-Syllable Words

Five-Syllable Words

Three-Syllable Words

e	mō	tion

Four-Syllable Words

WORKSHEET 21–F

Practice saying these similar groups of *tion* words to build up your speed. Notice that the accent is on the underlined syllable before *tion*.

ā *tion*	ā *tion*	ĭ *tion*
lo<u>ca</u>tion	ope<u>ra</u>tion	am<u>bi</u>tion
pro<u>ba</u>tion	quo<u>ta</u>tion	nu<u>tri</u>tion
foun<u>da</u>tion	transpor<u>ta</u>tion	pe<u>ti</u>tion
sal<u>va</u>tion	frus<u>tra</u>tion	con<u>di</u>tion
tax<u>a</u>tion	conser<u>va</u>tion	ig<u>ni</u>tion
trans<u>la</u>tion	cre<u>a</u>tion	par<u>ti</u>tion
vo<u>ca</u>tion	concen<u>tra</u>tion	cog<u>ni</u>tion
o<u>ra</u>tion	expor<u>ta</u>tion	mu<u>ni</u>tion
in<u>fla</u>tion	edu<u>ca</u>tion	e<u>di</u>tion
sen<u>sa</u>tion	illus<u>tra</u>tion	po<u>si</u>tion

When *tion* is added to a verb to make a noun, the accent changes to the syllable just before *tion*. Practice changing the accent as you read these words. The accented syllable has a box around it.

con|firm| → confir|ma|tion

ex|pect| → expec|ta|tion

ob|serve| → obser|va|tion

in|form| → infor|ma|tion

ex|plain| → expla|na|tion

con|sult| → consul|ta|tion

con|verse| → conver|sa|tion

WORKSHEET 21–G

All these verbs end in *ct* and all can be changed into nouns by adding the suffix *-ion*. Although we think of the ending as *-tion* because of the way we pronounce it, we are adding only *ion* to these words since *t* is the last letter of the root. Change these verbs into nouns. Then practice saying the words as fast as you can. Note that the accent is always on the syllable before *tion*.

Verb	Noun	Verb	Noun
inject	_____	* collect	_____
* correct	_____	reject	_____
* infect	_____	* perfect	_____
* object	_____	project	_____
* elect	_____	* direct	_____
* attract	_____	* deduct	_____
* subtract	_____	addict	_____
* construct	_____		

Have another student test you on spelling the starred words. They are practical spelling words.

My score: _____ words correct.

Proofing Practice: Two common List 21 words are misspelled in each of the sentences below. Correct them as shown.

1. The commotion in the police ~~stacian~~ *station* began when the chief's connection with corrupsion was announced.

2. The administration had no good explanation for the nasion's problem with inflacian.

3. She received confirmasion of her reservation in Grand Juncsion.

4. In her dissertation, Dr. Butler discussed her investigasion of the creation of a constellacian.

5. Mr. Travers signed the petition stating his objecsion to high taxation for transportasion.

Change the verbs (action words) listed below into *tion* words. Words that end in *tion* are always nouns (naming words). Be careful; you may have to add, drop, or change some letters before adding the ending. Use your dictionary.

Verb	Noun	Verb	Noun
promote	_____	*corrupt	_____
*frustrate	_____	starve	_____
*converse	_____	*inform	_____
act	_____	*prescribe	_____
quote	_____	*educate	_____
*explain	_____	*concentrate	_____
edit	_____	*subscribe	_____
*add	_____		

Fill in each blank with either the noun or verb form of the italicized word so that the sentence reads correctly.

1. Can you *add* the numbers correctly? It will be easier if you know your

   _____ facts.

2. Stuart has excellent *concentration*. He can _____ even when the television is on.

3. Alexandra will *explain* in detail how to change a tire. Listen carefully to her

   _____.

4. The doctor *prescribed* a new remedy for Jason's sore throat. The last

   _____ was not effective.

5. Megan should _____ to this magazine. She will receive a reduced rate for a two-year *subscription*.

Have another student test you on spelling the starred words. They are practical spelling words.

My score: _____ words correct.

Your teacher will dictate some practical spelling words from List 21. Repeat each word, count the syllables, and spell the word by syllables under the correct heading. Then write the whole word.

Two-Syllable Words

_____ + _____ = _____

_____ + _____ = _____

_____ + _____ = _____

Three-Syllable Words

_____ + _____ + _____ = _____

_____ + _____ + _____ = _____

_____ + _____ + _____ = _____

_____ + _____ + _____ = _____

_____ + _____ + _____ = _____

_____ + _____ + _____ = _____

Four-Syllable Words

_____ + _____ + _____ + _____ = _____

_____ + _____ + _____ + _____ = _____

Five-Syllable Words

_____ + _____ + _____ + _____ + _____ = _____

How many words with at least five letters can you make from the word CONGRATULATIONS? Score one point for each letter in the word. For two-syllable words, multiply your score by two; for three-syllable words, multiply by three. Example: *notation*—8 letters × 3 syllables = 24 points. Write the words below.

My score: _____

WORKSHEET 21–J

Fill in each blank with a word from below. Then complete the puzzle with the words you have used.

promotion   eruption   reception   nutrition   subscription

attention   commotion   ignition   explanation   transportation

1. To spell correctly, you must pay careful _____ to the sounds and syllables. (8 Across)

2. We congratulated the groom during the wedding _____. (5 Across)

3. Jadine's _____ to *Weekly News* magazine has run out. (1 Across)

4. The _____ in the hallway caused the principal to investigate the trouble. (6 Down)

5. What form of _____ will you use to get to California from New York? (3 Down)

6. Proper _____ is important to good health. You must eat balanced meals. (9 Across)

7. The _____ of Mount St. Helens caused significant damage in Washington. (4 Down)

8. Will you please explain the procedures again? I didn't follow your first

_____. (10 Across)

9. Alexander left his car keys in

the _____. (2 Down)

10. Juanita is due for a

_____ and pay raise next month. (7 Across)

All of the words below end in *tion*. Write the correct word next to its definition. Use a dictionary to look up the meaning of unfamiliar words.

inflation	deduction	auction	condensation
oration	contrition	ration	exportation
munition	petition	cognition	administration

1. A public sale of property to the highest bidder _____

2. The act or process of knowing _____

3. A fixed allowance or share of something _____

4. A formal, written request to those in authority _____

5. Military equipment and ammunition _____

6. Sincere repentance; penitence _____

7. An elaborate speech or sermon _____

8. Causes an increase in prices _____

9. The process of changing steam to water _____

10. The executive duties of a business _____

11. Sending goods out of the country for sale _____

12. Something that is subtracted or taken away _____

Unscramble the words below and spell them correctly in the blanks and circles. All the words can be found in the list above.

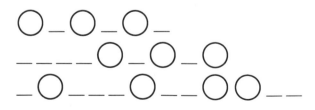

N O T A I R

D I D N O T C U E

D A N C E O N I T S O N

Unscramble the letters you have written in the circles to make another word from the list above:

— — — — — — — — — — —

WORKSHEET 21–L

Read the following sentences and circle all the List 21 words that you can find.

1. Did Mr. Chancellor mention the location of his new home?

2. The service station was in bad condition after the fire.

3. Adoption of pollution controls is very important.

4. Is there a solution to the problems caused by inflation?

5. Omar needed a prescription to buy medicine for his bad infection.

6. They will soon begin construction at a new location.

7. Judge Galloway demanded an inspection of all election returns.

8. Your interruption ruined my concentration.

9. Ms. Rudyard asked for an explanation of the tax investigation.

10. The administration of this office involves consultation with bankers.

Look at List 21. Choose five words and write them in sentences below.

_____

_____

_____

_____

_____

Take out a piece of blank paper. Your teacher will dictate three of the sentences above for you to write.

You have completed the worksheets for List 21. Now it is time to check your accuracy in reading and spelling. Read and spell ten words selected by your teacher, and record your scores on the Accuracy Checklist. Work toward 90–100 percent accuracy.

When you have achieved 90–100 percent accuracy in reading, build up your reading speed. Decide on your rate goal with your teacher. Record your rate on the Proficiency Graph.

My goal for reading List 21 is _____ words per minute with two or fewer errors.

LIST 22: *-sion* AND *-cian*

-sion = /shən/	*-sion* = /shən/	*-sion* = /zhən/	*-cian* = /shən/
* discussion	* tension	* vision	* optician
* depression	expansion	version	mortician
* session	* extension	* division	* musician
* mission	* comprehension	* decision	* physician
confession	suspension	supervision	technician
* admission	ascension	exclusion	logician
* recession	progression	* collision	magician
* permission	omission	* occasion	statistician
oppression	submission	transfusion	mathematician
concession	concussion	* revision	* politician
* impression	* commission	precision	* electrician
suppression	percussion	* television	
* expression	procession	* invasion	Exception
repression	* intermission	incision	* fashion
* profession	digression	fusion	
progression	propulsion	* explosion	
* transmission	compulsion	corrosion	
	expulsion	* conclusion	
	convulsion	* confusion	
	repulsion	diversion	
		excursion	
		conversion	
		submersion	

* Practical spelling words. The teacher and student should decide together how many of these words the student will be responsible for spelling.

28

WORKSHEET 22–A

Review: *-tion* is a common ending, which says /shən/.

-sion and *-cian* are two more endings that say /shən/.
-sion has a second sound, /zhən/.
Like *-tion* words, the syllable just before *-sion* and *-cian* is accented. Vowels that come just before *-sion* and *-cian* are long except for *i,* which always has a short sound, /ĭ/.

Draw a box around the accented syllable that comes just before *-sion* or *-cian*. Mark the vowel in the accented syllable. Then pronounce and combine the syllables to read the whole word.

-*sion* and -*cian* = /shən/				Copy
dis cus sion	discus̆sion			_____
im pres sion	impression			_____
o mis sion	omission			_____
pro ces sion	procession			_____
com pre hen sion	comprehension			_____
op ti cian	optician			_____
phy si cian	physician			_____
lo gi cian	logician			_____
stat is ti cian	statistician			_____

-*sion* = /zhən/			
di vi sion	division		_____
con clu sion	conclusion		_____
col li sion	collision		_____
in ci sion	incision		_____
con fu sion	confusion		_____
cor ro sion	corrosion		_____
ex cur sion	excursion		_____
di ver sion	diversion		_____

29

Unscramble these multisyllabic words. If you circle the *-sion* or *-cian* ending, you will know which syllable is last.

sion   pres   ex   _____   si   mu   cian   _____

trans   sion   fu   _____   tru   in   sion   _____

cian   si   phy   _____   sion   ex   plo   _____

trans   sion   mis   _____   per   sion   cus   _____

pan   ex   sion   _____   gi   ma   cian   _____

cian   ti   mor   _____   sion   ad   mis   _____

pre   com   sion   hen   _____

per   sion   vi   su   _____

i   cian   ti   pol   _____

cian   e   tri   lec   _____

vi   tel   sion   e   _____

sion   in   mis   ter   _____

Find and circle the eighteen words above in the puzzle below. The words can be found in a straight line across or up and down.

↓

```
A D M I S S I O N T H C O M P R E H E N S I O N E S Y L
L A U B L P O L I T I C I A N E B E X P R E S S I O N E
F O S U P E R V I S I O N G R E T H M O R T I C I A N E
E N I N T R U S I O N D I I N G T R A N S M I S S I O N
S T C I O N E L E C T R I C I A N E X P L O S I O N S I
O N I A N D T E L E V I S I O N C I A P H Y S I C I A N
N I A E X P A N S I O N S A A C T R A N S F U S I O N C
E I N T E R M I S S I O N N N P E R C U S S I O N T E D
```

Write the leftover letters in the blanks below. Start at the arrow and work from left to right.

___ ___ ___   ___ ___ ___ ___ ___ ___ ___   ___ ___ ___ ___ ___ ___   ___ ___ ___

___ ___ ___ ___ ___ ___ ___   -___ ___ ___ ___,   -___ ___ ___ ___,   ___ ___ ___

-___ ___ ___ ___   ___ ___   ___ ___ ___ ___ ___ ___ ___ ___.

WORKSHEET 22-C

-*sion* has two sounds, /shən/ and /zhən/. If you listen carefully, you can hear the difference and it will help you in spelling.

Pronounce the words; then copy them under the correct heading.
Hint: There will always be a vowel before the sound of /zhən/.

mis sion   ver sion   fu sion

ten sion   ses sion   vi sion

*oc ca sion   sup pres sion   o mis sion

*de ci sion   *per mis sion   as cen sion

*in va sion   *di vi sion   *pro fes sion

ex pan sion   pre ci sion   *ex pres sion

con cus sion   cor ro sion   *con fu sion

/shən/	/zhən/
1. _____	1. _____
2. _____	2. _____
3. _____	3. _____
4. _____	4. _____
5. _____	5. _____
6. _____	6. _____
7. _____	7. _____
8. _____	8. _____
9. _____	9. _____
10. _____	10. _____
11. _____	

Have another student test you on spelling the starred words. They are practical spelling words.

My score: _____ words correct.

WORKSHEET 22–D

Fill in the blanks with *sion* or *cian*. Then copy the whole word. Use *sion* after *s, n,* or *l,* or when it sounds like /zhən/. Use *cian* to name a person.

	Copy	ABC Order
tech ni _____	_____	_____
*oc ca _____	_____	_____
*pro fes _____	_____	_____
*de ci _____	_____	_____
ma gi _____	_____	_____
*in va _____	_____	_____
*per mis _____	_____	_____
*phy si _____	_____	_____
pro pul _____	_____	_____
mor ti _____	_____	_____
ex pan _____	_____	_____
*pol i ti _____	_____	_____

Now go back and write the words in alphabetical order.

Complete the following sentences with words from above that end in *cian*.

1. A person who performs magic tricks is a _____.

2. Another word for a medical doctor is _____.

3. A _____ is someone who holds political office.

4. A person skilled in the mechanical aspects of a trade is a _____.

5. A _____ is a funeral director.

Have another student test you on spelling the starred words. They are practical spelling words.

My score: _____ words correct.

WORKSHEET 22–E

Your teacher will dictate some words. Sound out each word as you write the missing syllable(s).
Then write the whole word, saying it aloud as you spell it.

	Copy	ABC Order
*1. _____ sion	_____	_____
*2. di _____ sion	_____	_____
*3. phy si _____	_____	_____
*4. _____ plo sion	_____	_____
*5. de _____ sion	_____	_____
*6. con _____ _____	_____	_____
7. _____ gi _____	_____	_____
*8. _____ fes _____	_____	_____
9. _____ _____ sion	_____	_____
10. cor _____ _____	_____	_____

-ission Words

*11. _____ sion	_____	_____
*12. _____ _____ _____	_____	_____
*13. _____ _____ _____	_____	_____
*14. _____ _____ _____	_____	_____
*15. _____ _____ _____ _____	_____	_____

Now go back and write the words in alphabetical order.

Have another student test you on spelling the starred words. They are practical spelling words.

My score: _____ words correct.

Divide these words into syllables. Mark the long and short vowels and pronounce the words. Remember that *i* before *sion* or *cian* always has a short sound. The accented syllable has a box around it.

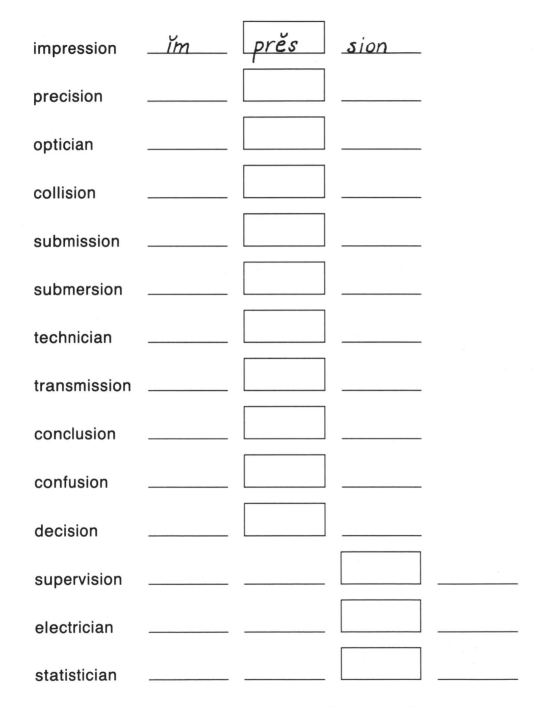

impression	ĭm	prĕs	sion
precision			
optician			
collision			
submission			
submersion			
technician			
transmission			
conclusion			
confusion			
decision			
supervision			
electrician			
statistician			

If you say the words aloud and listen carefully, you can hear -*sion* say /zhǝn/. Put a star by seven words that end in /zhǝn/. (Hint: These words have either a vowel or the letter *r* just before *sion*.)

34

WORKSHEET 22–G

The following *sion* words contain the Latin roots *cess, press,* and *miss*. Although we think of the ending as *sion* because of the way we pronounce it, we are adding only the suffix *-ion* to these words since they end in *ss*. Circle the Latin roots. Practice reading these words to build up your speed.

-cession	*-pression*	*-mission*
suc(cess)ion	compression	omission
procession	oppression	commission
recession	impression	permission
intercession	depression	admission
concession	suppression	submission
secession	expression	transmission
	repression	intermission

When *-sion* says /zhǝn/, it often follows a short-*i* sound. Draw a box around the accented syllable that comes just before *-sion* and mark the vowel. Build up your reading speed on these words.

[vĭ]sion   revision   division   precision   supervision

decision   incision   collision   provision

Complete the puzzle with the nine nouns above. Start with the shortest and longest words, and then you will be able to determine where the other words fit.

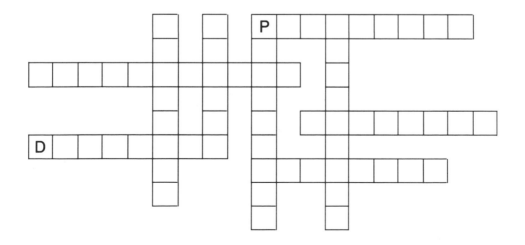

35

WORKSHEET 22–H

Change the following words into nouns (naming words) by adding *ion*. Note that there will be two *s*'s in the middle of the words.

process   *procession*   *impress   _____

*discuss   _____   *profess   _____

repress   _____   *depress   _____

*express   _____   confess   _____

*recess   _____   suppress   _____

For the following words, change the final *t* to *s* and add *sion*.

*permit   _____   *admit   _____

*transmit   _____   omit   _____

submit   _____   *commit   _____

Fill in each blank with the correct *-sion* or *-cian* word.

1. One who plays <u>music</u> is a _____.*

2. When you <u>divide</u>, you do _____.*

3. A person involved in <u>politics</u> is a _____.*

4. When you finally <u>decide</u>, you make a _____.*

5. If you are <u>confused</u>, you experience _____.*

6. When a bomb <u>explodes</u>, there is an _____.*

7. One who performs <u>magic</u> is a _____.*

8. When two cars <u>collide</u>, there is a _____.*

Have another student test you on spelling the starred words. They are practical spelling words.

My score: _____ words correct.

Review: *i* before *sion* or *cian* always has a _____ sound.

36

WORKSHEET 22–I

Your teacher will dictate practical spelling words from List 22. Repeat each word aloud, decide which column it belongs in, and spell the word, sounding each syllable aloud.

-sion = /shən/ (Names a condition; follows *s* or *n*)	*-cian* = /shən/ (Names a person; follows a vowel)	*-sion* = /zhən/ (Follows a vowel or *r*)
_____	_____	_____
_____	_____	_____
_____	_____	_____
_____	_____	_____
_____		_____
_____		_____
_____		_____

There is an important exception to spelling the /shən/ ending. Practice spelling *fashion,* and then write it in a sentence.

fashion → fa _____ ion → f ___ sh _____ n

_____ sh _____ → f _____ → _____

_____

_____

Proofing Practice: Two common List 22 words are misspelled in each of the sentences below. Correct them as shown.

1. The students experienced a great deal of ~~tention~~ *tension* before taking the math test on long

   divizion.

2. By profeshen, Andrea is a phizishn.

3. Our class had an interesting discusion about the telavizun special on drug abuse.

37

WORKSHEET 22–J

Complete the puzzle with the words below. You may use your dictionary.

conversion	exclusion	commission	diversion
precision	repulsion	incision	mortician
technician	excursion	optician	compulsion

Across

3. The state of being left out or excluded

5. Forcing someone to do something; a strong urge to act a certain way

6. Changing something from one thing to another; the experience of becoming religious

9. A cut or gash

10. The quality of being exact or accurate

11. A feeling of extreme dislike and rejection

Down

1. One who makes and fits eyeglasses

2. One skilled in the details of a trade

3. A pleasure trip; a short journey

4. Extra money paid to salespeople for selling

7. Something that relaxes and amuses; a sport or pastime

8. An undertaker

WORKSHEET 22–K

Read the following story. Circle all the words that contain *tion, sion,* or *cian*. Write them at the bottom of the page under the appropriate heading.

I must make a confession—all I did last weekend was watch television. I wasn't suffering from depression; I simply had no ambition to do anything else. Perhaps this was because my physician gave me two injections and a blood transfusion, which gave me a weird sensation.

Certainly, I had no expectations that the "tube" would give me great satisfaction, but it did offer some diversion. I watched a funny movie about a musician's frustration while trying to explain his love for jazz to a cranky mortician. I guess you should avoid the compulsion, however strong, to force your convictions on others.

In addition, I watched an educational program about the investigation of several politicians who had been involved in fiscal corruption. My conclusion was that both invasion of privacy and extortion had taken place.

tion	*cian*	*sion*
_____	_____	_____
_____	_____	_____
_____	_____	_____
_____		_____
_____		_____
_____		_____
_____		_____
_____		
_____		
_____		

WORKSHEET 22–L

Complete each sentence with a word from below that makes sense in the sentence.

admission   magician   comprehension   optician   explosion   permission

vision   decision   transmission   confusion   discussion

1. The bundle of dynamite caused a huge _____.

2. Gabe and Rebecca watched an amazing _____ perform tricks at the fair.

3. Make sure you understand the story because Ms. Brewster is going to test your _____ tomorrow.

4. Oscar led an interesting _____ in civics class the other day.

5. Something major is wrong with my car. I'll have to get the _____ checked.

6. May I have your _____ to borrow this book?

7. Peter Sawyer's _____ to quit smoking was intelligent.

8. There was so much _____ in the office that no one could get any work done.

9. This year the price of _____ to the circus is six dollars.

10. Elmer's _____ has gotten so bad that he must go to the _____ to get eyeglasses.

Proofing Practice: Two common List 22 words are misspelled in each of the sentences below. Correct them as shown.

1. The concession stand was open during ~~intermiscian~~ *intermission* of the percusscian concert.

2. The magician on televizion made quite an imprecian on the electrician.

3. The optision checked the physician's vizian.

4. Dennis needed a physician's permiscian for admission to the deprescian clinic.

WORKSHEET 22–M

Read the following sentences and circle all the List 22 words that you can find.

1. Dr. Karwan, the optician, suffers from blurry vision.

2. Esther's physician asked permission to give her a transfusion.

3. A television technician came to the mansion to repair the faulty transmission.

4. The musician played with expression during the recording session.

5. Jennifer's admission to the law profession was a special occasion.

6. The mortician had her work cut out for her after the explosion.

7. The mathematician suffered confusion and depression after the collision.

8. The logician came to the conclusion that the politician had made a wise decision.

9. The awkward physician was not able to make the incision with precision.

10. Give me permission to bring this discussion about tax evasion to a conclusion.

Look at List 22. Choose five words and write them in sentences below.

_____

_____

_____

_____

_____

Take out a piece of blank paper. Your teacher will dictate three of the sentences above for you to write.

You have completed the worksheets for List 22. Now it is time to check your accuracy in reading and spelling. Read and spell ten words selected by your teacher, and record your scores on the Accuracy Checklist. Work toward 90–100 percent accuracy.

When you have achieved 90–100 percent accuracy in reading, build up your reading speed. Decide on your rate goal with your teacher. Record your rate on the Proficiency Graph.

My goal for reading List 22 is _____ words per minute with two or fewer errors.

LIST 23: *-ous* AND *-age*

-ous	*-ous*	*-age*	*-age*
* nervous	* joyous	* message	* baggage
* generous	wondrous	* courage	cribbage
* tremendous	ominous	* damage	rummage
scandalous	marvelous	cottage	cabbage
rigorous	* humorous	* village	passage
thunderous	* enormous	* luggage	* postage
courageous	numerous	shortage	* bandage
prosperous	hazardous	* manage	* package
unanimous	disastrous	savage	voltage
mountainous	traitorous	portage	* garbage
miraculous	anonymous	* language	storage
* jealous	* dangerous	* advantage	voyage
mischievous	lecherous	* average	mortgage
pompous	monotonous	image	sausage
* fabulous	ruinous		
* famous	monstrous		
outrageous	advantageous		

* Practical spelling words. The teacher and student should decide together how many of these words the student will be responsible for spelling.

WORKSHEET 23–A

-ous is a schwa ending that says /əs/.
-age is an ending that says /ĭj/.

Pronounce and combine the syllables. Then cover the divided word and practice reading the whole word. Underline the *-ous* or *-age* ending in the whole word.

ner vous	nerv<u>ous</u>	mess age	mess<u>age</u>
pom pous	pompous	dam age	damage
joy ous	joyous	vil lage	village
por ous	porous	short age	shortage
jeal ous	jealous	man age	manage
fab u lous	fabulous	sav age	savage
e nor mous	enormous	wreck age	wreckage
dis as trous	disastrous	ban dage	bandage
mar vel ous	marvelous	cab bage	cabbage
tre men dous	tremendous	bag gage	baggage
hu mor ous	humorous	gar bage	garbage
gen er ous	generous	cot tage	cottage
out rage ous	outrageous	sau sage	sausage
nu mer ous	numerous	im age	image
ru in ous	ruinous	ad van tage	advantage
		av er age	average

u nan i mous	unanimous
mir a cu lous	miraculous
a non y mous	anonymous

ad van tage ous	advantageous
mo not o nous	monotonous

43

Your teacher will dictate some words. Sound out each word as you write the missing syllable(s). Then write the whole word, saying it aloud as you spell it.

	Copy	ABC Order
1. _____ mous	_____	_____
2. fab ___ _____	_____	_____
3. _____ vel _____	_____	_____
4. ___ _____ mous	_____	_____
5. _____ er _____	_____	_____
6. _____ bage	_____	_____
7. sav _____	_____	_____
8. av _____ age	_____	_____
9. _____ age	_____	_____
10. _____ _____ tage	_____	_____

Bonus: Four-syllable words

___ _____ ___ mous   _____

_____ not o _____   _____

a _____ y _____   _____

Add either *ous* or *age* to make a word. Then write the word.

post_____	_____	jeal_____	_____
nerv_____	_____	man_____	_____
joy_____	_____	saus_____	_____
wondr_____	_____	fam_____	_____
mess_____	_____	dam_____	_____

Now go back and write the words at the top of the page in alphabetical order.

WORKSHEET 23–C

-ous and *-age* are unaccented endings. The accent falls on another syllable in the word.

Divide these words into syllables, noting the accent patterns.

Accent the First Syllable

manage [ ] _____

famous [ ] _____

package [ ] _____

image [ ] _____

courage [ ] _____

jealous [ ] _____

savage [ ] _____

Accent the First Syllable

generous [ ] _____ _____

average [ ] _____ _____

humorous [ ] _____ _____

dangerous [ ] _____ _____

fabulous [ ] _____ _____

prosperous [ ] _____ _____

hazardous [ ] _____ _____

Accent the Second Syllable

advantage _____ [ ] _____

enormous _____ [ ] _____

outrageous _____ [ ] _____

Accent the Second Syllable

tremendous _____ [ ] _____

disastrous _____ [ ] _____

Review these accent patterns.

__´__   The accent is usually on the _____ syllable in two-syllable words.

__´____   The accent is usually on the _____ syllable in three-syllable words.

____´__   The accent is usually on the _____ syllable in three-syllable words that contain a prefix, root, and suffix.

45

WORKSHEET 23–D

Can you figure out the following words? If you hear a single consonant sound in the middle of the word, be sure to double the consonant to keep the first vowel short. Put a check after the nine words that have double middle consonants.

Copy

1. A small town   *vi __ __ age   _____

2. Fee for mailing letters   *po __ __ age   _____

3. A written note   *me __ __ age   _____

4. A type of sale   ru __ __ age   _____

5. A small house   co __ __ age   _____

6. Trash   *ga __ __ age   _____

7. A game played with cards   cri __ __ age   _____

8. Electrical force   vo __ __ age   _____

9. Used for travel   *lu __ __ age   _____

10. Used for travel   *ba __ __ age   _____

11. A type of vegetable   ca __ __ age   _____

12. Not enough, a lack   *sho __ __ age   _____

13. Cloth strip for a wound   *ba __ __ age   _____

14. A hall; a way to go   *pa __ __ age   _____

Remember these exceptions to the spelling generalization above.

     *damage   *manage   savage

Make up a sentence that includes all three of them.

_____

_____

Have another student test you on spelling the starred words. They are practical spelling words.

My score: _____ words correct.

Add *ous* to each noun to make an adjective.

Noun	Adjective	ABC Order
danger	*dangerous*	
scandal		
marvel		
thunder		
pomp		
peril		
humor		
traitor		
joy		
ruin		
hazard		

The words below are tricky. One or more letters need to be changed before you add *ous*. Check your word list or dictionary if necessary.

Noun	Adjective	ABC Order
nerve		
fame		
pore		
mischief		
disaster		
monster		
wonder		
miracle		

Now go back and write the words in each section in alphabetical order.

WORKSHEET 23–F

Your teacher will dictate some words. Say the words aloud and write them in the correct column.

ous   *age*

_____   _____
_____   _____
_____   _____
_____   _____
_____   _____
_____   _____

The words below are tricky because they are not spelled exactly as they sound. Practice them and pay attention to the tricky parts.

mort gage   mor__gage   av er age   av__ __age
 /mor´ gĭj/   mor__ __age   /ăv´ rĭj/   a__ __ra__ __

                    — — — — — — —   — — — — — — —

lan gu age   lan__ __age
 /lăng´ wĭj/   l__ __g__age
                    l__n__ __age

                    — — — — — — — — —

Proofing Practice: Two common List 23 words are misspelled in each of the sentences below. Correct them as shown.

    dangerous
1. The ~~dangerus~~ trip to the villige made us nervous and anxious.

2. Samantha is jealus of the prosperous and famous morgage banker.

3. The arrival of an anonymus message at our summer cottige seemed ominous.

4. It took great courige to cross the hazardus passage at night.

5. My sister put the rotten cabbage and sausige in the garbij.

48

-eous usually says /ē əs/. The accent is always on the syllable just before /ē əs/.

Draw a box around the accented syllable. Then write the whole word.

/ē əs/	Copy	ABC Order
☐hid☐ e ous	*hideous*	_____
cour te ous	_____	_____
dis cour te ous	_____	_____
spon ta ne ous	_____	_____
si mul ta ne ous	_____	_____
mis cel la ne ous	_____	_____
in stan ta ne ous	_____	_____

-geous breaks this pattern and says /jəs/. The accent is on the syllable just before /jəs/. Draw a box around the accented syllable. Then write the whole word.

/jəs/	Copy	ABC Order
gor geous	_____	_____
cour a geous	_____	_____
out ra geous	_____	_____
ad van ta geous	_____	_____

Now go back and write the words in each section in alphabetical order.

Find and circle the eleven words above in the puzzle below. The words can be found in a straight line across or up and down.

```
G V H M I S C I N S T A N T A N E O U S P O
O D I S C O U R T E O U S A D V A U D I S C
R A D V A N T A G E O U S G O R G E O U S U
G R E D I S S I M U L T A N E O U S M I S C
E P O U T R A G E O U S C O U R A G E O U S
C O U R T E O U S S P O N T A N E O U S I M
M I S C E L L A N E O U S O U T R A G E O U
```

-ous is an adjective ending. All words ending in *ous* are adjectives (describing words).

Write the correct *ous* word in each blank.

1. Full of danger   _____

2. Full of peril   _____

3. Full of hazards   _____

4. Full of mountains   _____

5. Full of humor   _____

6. Full of wonder   _____

7. Full of joy   _____

8. Full of mischief   _____

Did you remember to change the *f* in *mischief* to *v* before adding *ous*? _____

Write the correct *ous* word in each blank. Choose from the words at the bottom of the page. Use your dictionary if you are not sure of the meanings.

1. Everyone voted for Howard for president. The vote was _____.

2. It was a _____ act to run into the burning house and rescue the child.

3. Everyone thought it was _____ that the police officer had accepted the bribe.

4. It was very _____ of Mr. Espinosa to give a one-thousand-dollar gift to the Boy Scouts.

5. Ms. Savage's business was very _____; she made an enormous profit each month.

6. He wished to remain _____; he did not want people to know who he was.

anonymous	scandalous	courageous	generous
unanimous			prosperous

Complete the sentences with words from below. Write the words in the puzzle.

sausage	package	cottage	advantage	damage
portage	garbage	average	language	courage
voyage	manage	mortgage	cabbage	savage
postage				passage

1. Ms. Taylor's monthly (15 Across) payment on the house is well above the (6 Down) that most people paid five years ago.
2. Do you have enough (3 Down) to crawl through the secret (9 Down) by yourself?
3. Victor would like to learn to speak a foreign (5 Down).
4. We will have to (2 Down) our canoe. Can you (13 Across) the heavy end?
5. The (11 Across) of an overseas (12 Across) by ship is that you don't feel jet lag.
6. Will you please take out the (14 Across)?
7. Three (8 Across) animals at the zoo escaped and caused a lot of (10 Down) to the grounds.
8. When you go to the grocery store, please pick up a pound of (1 Down) and a head of (4 Down).
9. The (7 Down) for mailing the (2 Across) was outrageous!
10. The Brewsters and Goddards rented a (4 Across) by the lake for three weeks last summer.

WORKSHEET 23-J

Read the following sentences and circle all the List 23 words that you can find.

1. Ms. Lopez put her luggage in the baggage room for storage during her voyage.

2. The raccoon rummaged through the garbage and ate some cabbage and sausage.

3. It may be dangerous to travel among savages if you don't speak their language.

4. The gorgeous singer was jealous of the famous movie star.

5. The passage in the book was not humorous; in fact, it was very monotonous.

6. The prosperous gentleman was both generous and courageous.

7. Graduation is a joyous, wondrous, and marvelous time.

8. Ginger's message gave me the courage to lead the hazardous invasion.

9. A disastrous flood caused damage to the cottages in the mountainous village.

10. Edward cannot afford the postage for that package.

11. The mischievous child taped bandages all over the cribbage board.

Look at List 23. Choose five words and write them in sentences below.

_____

_____

_____

_____

_____

Take out a piece of blank paper. Your teacher will dictate three of the sentences above for you to write.

You have completed the worksheets for List 23. Now it is time to check your accuracy in reading and spelling. Read and spell ten words selected by your teacher, and record your scores on the Accuracy Checklist. Work toward 90–100 percent accuracy.

When you have achieved 90–100 percent accuracy in reading, build up your reading speed. Decide on your rate goal with your teacher. Record your rate on the Proficiency Graph.

My goal for reading List 23 is _____ words per minute with two or fewer errors.

LIST 24: -ture, -tu-, AND -sure

-ture = /chər/	-ture = /chər/	-tu- = /cho͞o/	-sure = /zhər/
* picture	* furniture	statue	* measure
* future	* departure	* fortune	leisure
* capture	agriculture	virtue	pleasure
* nature	* adventure	mutual	exposure
* lecture	* temperature	Portugal	composure
* moisture	* signature	ritual	* treasure
torture	* manufacture	punctual	
culture	* literature	spatula	-sure = /shər/
* creature	curvature	situate	pressure
structure	overture	punctuate	censure
puncture	expenditure	fluctuate	
gesture	legislature	* actual	
pasture	horticulture	impetuous	
feature	miniature	tarantula	
posture	caricature	congratulate	
venture	forfeiture	perpetual	
vulture	architecture	infatuate	
mixture	saturate	spiritual	
scripture	century	habitual	
fixture	natural	intellectual	
nurture			
fracture			
texture			
rupture			

* Practical spelling words. The teacher and student should decide together how many of these words the student will be responsible for spelling.

WORKSHEET 24-A

-ture is an ending that says /chər/.
-sure is an ending that says /zhər/ or /shər/.
-tu- comes in the middle of words and says /cho͞o/.

Pronounce and combine the syllables to read the whole word. Underline *-ture*, *-sure*, or *-tu-*.

-ture = /chər/

pic	ture			pic<u>ture</u>
fu	ture			future
na	ture			nature
lec	ture			lecture
mois	ture			moisture
tor	ture			torture
fur	ni	ture		furniture
ad	ven	ture		adventure
de	par	ture		departure
sig	na	ture		signature
ag	ri	cul	ture	agriculture
man	u	fac	ture	manufacture
hor	ti	cul	ture	horticulture
lit	er	a	ture	literature

-sure = /shər/

pres	sure	pressure
cen	sure	censure

-sure = /zhər/

mea	sure		measure
lei	sure		leisure
plea	sure		pleasure
ex	po	sure	exposure
com	po	sure	composure

-tu- = /cho͞o/

sta	tue			statue
vir	tue			virtue
for	tune			fortune
rĭ	tu	al		ritual
punc	tu	al		punctual
spă	tu	la		spatula
sĭ	tu	ate		situate
punc	tu	ate		punctuate
ac	tu	al		actual
im	pĕ	tu	ous	impetuous
ta	ran	tu	la	tarantula
con	gră	tu	late	congratulate
per	pĕ	tu	al	perpetual

54

WORKSHEET 24–B

Your teacher will dictate some words. Sound out each word as you write the missing syllable(s). Then write the whole word, saying it aloud as you spell it.

Copy

1. _____ ture   _____

2. mix _____   _____

3. _____ ture   _____

4. _____ ture   _____

5. _____ ven _____   _____

6. _____ _____ ture   _____

7. _____ _____ ture   _____

8. _____ na _____   _____

9. _____ _____ a _____   _____

10. ag _____ cul _____   _____

11. _____ u _____ _____   _____

12. _____ ti _____ _____   _____

Add *sure* to the word beginnings below. Then copy the words and put them in alphabetical order.

	Copy	ABC Order
mea_____	_____	_____
pres_____	_____	_____
plea_____	_____	_____
expo_____	_____	_____
compo_____	_____	_____
cen_____	_____	_____

-sure says /shər/ in two of the words above. Which ones are they? _____ and

_____ .

WORKSHEET 24–C

The /k/ sound before *-ture* or *-tu-* is always spelled with *c*.

End the incomplete syllable with *c*, add *ture,* and copy the whole word, saying the sounds aloud as you spell.

	Copy			Copy
pi____ _____	_____	pun____ _____	_____
le____ _____	_____	fra____ _____	_____
stru____ _____	_____	man u fa____ _____	_____

End the incomplete syllable with *c,* add *tu,* and copy the whole word, saying the sounds aloud as you spell.

	Copy			Copy
a____ _____al	_____	pun____ _____ate	_____
pun____ _____al	_____	flu____ _____ate	_____

Fill in the blanks with *tu*. Then copy the words, saying the sounds aloud as you spell.

	Copy	ABC Order
spa_____la	_____	_____
taran_____la	_____	_____
ri_____al	_____	_____
si_____ate	_____	_____
fluc_____ate	_____	_____
mu_____al	_____	_____
punc_____al	_____	_____
ac_____al	_____	_____

Now go back and write the words in the last section in alphabetical order.

56

WORKSHEET 24-D

-ture and *-sure* are unaccented endings. The accent falls on another syllable in the word.

Divide these words into syllables, noting the accent patterns.

Accent the First Syllable

gesture [   ] _____

feature [   ] _____

moisture [   ] _____

future [   ] _____

censure [   ] _____

Accent the First Syllable

signature [   ] _____ _____

furniture [   ] _____ _____

Accent the Second Syllable

departure _____ [   ] _____

adventure _____ [   ] _____

Divide these four-syllable words and note their accent patterns.

agriculture [   ] _____ _____ _____

temperature [   ] _____ _____ _____

literature [   ] _____ _____ _____

expenditure _____ [   ] _____ _____

manufacture _____ _____ [   ] _____

Review: Draw a line from the accent pattern to the rule describing it.

— ´ — The accent is usually on the second syllable in three-syllable words that contain a prefix, root, and suffix.

— ´ — — The accent is usually on the first syllable in two-syllable words.

— — ´ — The accent is usually on the first syllable in three-syllable words.

WORKSHEET 24-E

Write these words in the correct column, as shown.

sculpture	* actual	* fortune	* picture
exposure	composure	pressure	* lecture
Portugal	* treasure	* congratulate	* nature

ture	*sure*	*tu*
sculpture	_____	_____
_____	_____	_____
_____	_____	_____
_____	_____	_____

Add the correct ending. If you hear /chər/ at the end, add *ture*. If you hear /shər/ or /zhər/ at the end, add *sure*.

* mea_____	expo_____	* signa_____
lei_____	mois_____	* manufac_____
* crea_____	* plea_____	* tempera_____
		* adven_____

Have another student test you on spelling the starred words. They are practical spelling words.

My score: _____ words correct.

Proofing Practice: Two common List 24 words are misspelled in each of the sentences below. Correct them as shown.

temperature

1. The ~~temperatur~~ in Portugal does not flucchuate much in summer.

2. That statue is a real treazher; it must have cost a forchoon.

3. The legislature's acchual expenditure for agriculcher was $4,000.

4. Ms. Arby gave a lectur on mineature furniture.

5. Do you think there is a better future in architekcher or horticulcher?

58

WORKSHEET 24-F

Fill in each blank with a word from below that makes sense in the sentence. Then complete the puzzle.

1. A _____ is a picture or cartoon that makes fun of someone.
   (10 Across)

2. In Beverly's _____ time, she likes to watch television.
   (9 Across)

3. A _____ is a big, hairy spider.
   (7 Across)

4. Albert bent over too much; his _____ was not good.
   (5 Down)

5. When Eleanor's appendix _____, her physician had to operate.
   (4 Down)

6. The foster parents _____ the child as if it were their own.
   (3 Down)

7. Julio carved the _____ furniture for the doll house.
   (2 Across)

8. They called her a _____ drunkard because she was always drunk.
   (8 Across)

9. The captors _____ the spy until he gave them the secret information.
   (6 Across)

10. Walter used a _____ to remove the scrambled eggs from the pan.
    (1 Down)

ruptured	nurtured	leisure	tarantula	caricature
posture	habitual	spatula	tortured	miniature

Review:

-__ __ __ __ is an ending that says /chər/.   -__ __ __ __ is an ending that says /shər/ or /zhər/.

-__ __- comes in the middle of words and says /choo/.

59

WORKSHEET 24–G

Write the correct word from below next to its definition.

venture   mutual   censure   saturate   perpetual

impetuous   overture   gesture   fluctuate   horticulture

1. Lasting forever   _____

2. The science of growing flowers   _____

3. A risky or daring undertaking   _____

4. To rise and fall; to change continually   _____

5. Acting hastily, rashly, or with sudden feeling   _____

6. Done, said, felt, etc., by each toward the other   _____

7. A proposal or offer; a musical composition played by the orchestra as an introduction   _____

8. A motion of the body used instead of words or with words to help express an idea or feeling   _____

9. Find fault with; blame; criticize   _____

10. To soak thoroughly   _____

Complete each sentence with one of the words above.

1. The springtime temperature _____s a lot in Vermont. Some days it's warm and sunny; other days it's cold and windy.

2. The *William Tell* _____ is a famous piece of music and was the theme song for *The Lone Ranger* television program.

3. Lynna dislikes Christopher, and he says the feeling is _____.

4. Ms. Sheldrake uses her hands when she talks. Her _____s complement her verbal expression.

5. I don't care to _____ out in the snow today. Driving will be hazardous.

6. Richard tends to be an _____ person. He often makes hasty decisions without considering the consequences.

WORKSHEET 24-H

Read the following sentences and circle all the List 24 words that you can find.

1. Dr. Wong likes pictures of statues and structures from the fifteenth century.

2. The professor kept her composure as she read the scripture.

3. If you make good posture habitual, you won't have curvature of the spine.

4. The general lectured his men and told them not to torture any of the prisoners they captured.

5. I wonder if the temperature in Portugal fluctuates tremendously in winter.

6. When Mr. Adler saw the tarantula in the kitchen, he hit it with a spatula.

7. That creature in the pasture is a vulture.

8. The school's yearly expenditure for furniture was $700.

9. I want to congratulate you on your election to the legislature.

10. Punctuate the last sentence, and then add your signature.

Look at List 24. Choose five words and write them in sentences below.

_____

_____

_____

_____

_____

Take out a piece of blank paper. Your teacher will dictate three of the sentences above for you to write.

You have completed the worksheets for List 24. Now it is time to check your accuracy in reading and spelling. Read and spell ten words selected by your teacher, and record your scores on the Accuracy Checklist. Work toward 90–100 percent accuracy.

When you have achieved 90–100 percent accuracy in reading, build up your reading speed. Decide on your rate goal with your teacher. Record your rate on the Proficiency Graph.

My goal for reading List 24 is _____ words per minute with two or fewer errors.

LIST 25: SUFFIXES *-able* AND *-ible* AND CONSONANT-*le*

-able	*-ible*	Consonant-*le*
* portable	* possible	rectangle
* profitable	* terrible	* assemble
* comfortable	sensible	embezzle
* vegetable	* eligible	* example
excitable	* responsible	participle
* valuable	* visible	disciple
* capable	flexible	popsicle
* probable	legible	* miracle
liable	defensible	particle
applicable	forcible	multiple
* considerable	tangible	* motorcycle
admirable	divisible	honeysuckle
* adorable	collectible	* article
durable	audible	* icicle
desirable	negligible	cuticle
comparable	invincible	oracle
preventable	plausible	tricycle
navigable	reducible	cubicle
usable	intelligible	* bicycle
* variable	* deductible	* vehicle
dispensable	permissible	soluble
educable	accessible	obstacle
imaginable	reversible	receptacle
* suitable	resistible	bamboozle
	* incredible	

* Practical spelling words. The teacher and student should decide together how many of these words the student will be responsible for spelling.

-able and *-ible* are endings that say /əbl/.

Pronounce and combine the syllables. Then cover the divided word and practice reading the whole word.

pos	si	ble			possible
li	a	ble			liable
com	for	ta	ble		comfortable
val	u	a	ble		valuable
de	duc	ti	ble		deductible
el	i	gi	ble		eligible
ad	mi	ra	ble		admirable
in	tel	li	gi	ble	intelligible

Review: A C*le* syllable (C*le*) is a final syllable. The *e* is silent, and the syllable sounds like consonant-/əl/ *(table, jungle)*.

Vowels before a C*le* syllable in three- and four-syllable words usually have a schwa or short-*i* sound. Look for an exception in the list below.

cu	ti	cle	cuticle
ob	sta	cle	obstacle
i	ci	cle	icicle
dis	ci	ple	disciple
ve	hi	cle	vehicle
sol	u	ble	soluble

The word that does not have a schwa or short-*i* sound just before the C*le* syllable is

_____.

Your teacher will dictate some words. Sound out each word as you write the missing syllable(s). Then copy the word by syllables in the appropriate boxes below.

1. _____ si ble

2. _____ am _____

3. i _____ cle

4. _____ e ta _____

5. _____ ti _____

6. _____ u a ble

7. _____ i a ble

8. bi _____ cle

9. ter _____ ble

10. _____ pa _____

11. _____ _____ cle

12. _____ _____ si ble

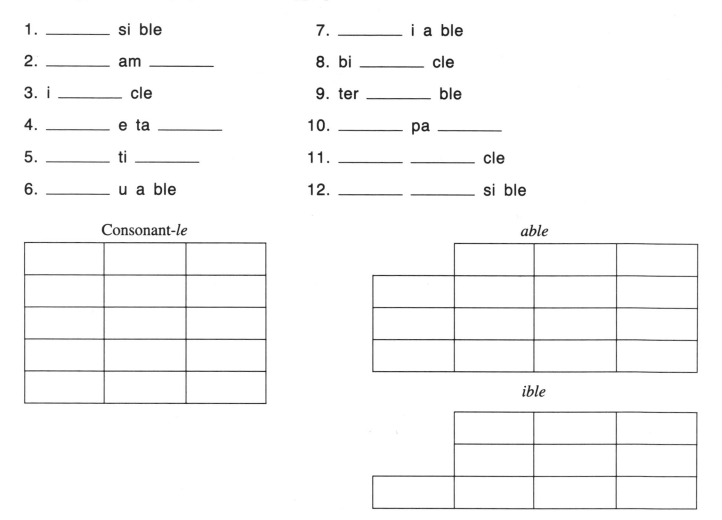

Consonant-*le*

able

ible

Unscramble the syllables to make recognizable words. If you circle the ending, you will know which syllable is last.

a   ble   dur   _____

cle   bi   cu   _____

tan   gle   rec   _____

tor   mo   cle   cy _____

flex   ble   i   _____

cle   ob   sta   _____

ble   vis   i   _____

for   ta   ble   com _____

WORKSHEET 25–C

-able and *-ible* are unaccented endings. The accent is on another syllable.
In C*le* words the accent is also on another syllable.

Divide these words into syllables, noting the accent patterns.

Accent the First Syllable

durable ____ ____ _____

visible ____ ____ _____

miracle ____ ____ _____

multiple ____ ____ _____

bicycle ____ ____ _____

flexible ____ ____ _____

Accent the First Syllable

educable ____ ____ _____

variable ____ ____ _____

navigable ____ ____ _____

motorcycle ____ ____ _____

eligible ____ ____ _____

profitable ____ ____ _____

Accent the Second Syllable

assemble _____ ____ _____

example _____ ____ _____

embezzle _____ ____ _____

bamboozle _____ ____ _____

Accent the Second Syllable

adorable _____ ____ ____

deductible _____ ____ ____

invincible _____ ____ ____

excitable _____ ____ ____

receptacle _____ ____ ____

divisible _____ ____ ____

reliable _____ ____ ____

WORKSHEET 25–D

When *i* precedes a consonant-*le* final syllable, it usually has a short sound. Practice reading the words below to build up your speed.

i says /ĭ/	ar ti cle	ve hi cle	cu ti cle
	pop si cle	i ci cle	par ti cle
	cu bi cle	mul ti ple	
i says /ī/	dis ci ple		
y says /ĭ/	bi cy cle	tri cy cle	
y says /ī/	mo tor cy cle		

Divide the consonant-*le* words below into syllables. Mark the long and short vowels and pronounce the words.

			Consonant-*le*
embezzle	ĕm	bĕz	zle
example	_____	_____	_____
obstacle	_____	_____	_____
assemble	_____	_____	_____
soluble	_____	_____	_____
miracle	_____	_____	_____
rectangle	_____	_____	_____
receptacle	_____	_____	_____	_____
participle	_____	_____	_____	_____

Review: Two endings that say /əbl/ are _____ and _____. Give an example for each of these endings: _____ and _____.

Learn this spelling pattern:
   ation becomes *able* (*application* ↔ *applicable*).
If words end in *ation*, their related /əbl/ form will be spelled *able*, not *ible*.

Change these *ation* nouns to *able* adjectives and vice versa.

Nouns		Adjectives
application	↔	*applicable*
_____	↔	vegetable (also a noun)
excitation	↔	_____
_____	↔	navigable
demonstration	↔	_____
habitation	↔	_____
_____	↔	considerable
_____	↔	educable
adoration	↔	_____
duration	↔	_____
variation	↔	_____
_____	↔	imaginable
_____	↔	dispensable

Choose the correct form of the words listed below to complete the sentences.

1. Give some _____ to taking this position. It would mean a

   _____ raise in salary.

   considerable—consideration

2. Complete the _____ by including any past experience that would

   be _____ to this job.

   applicable—application

WORKSHEET 25-F

If you can change an /əbl/ word to a word that ends in *ition, sion,* or *ive,* use *ible* to spell /əbl/.
    If you hear divis<u>ə</u>ble,
        think   divisi<u>o</u>n.
    Then spell divis<u>i</u>ble.

Change the words below to *ible* words. Check your dictionary if you need to.

                                    ible

depression ⟶   <u>*depressible*</u>

defensive ⟶   _____

responsive ⟶   * _____

vision ⟶   * _____

audition ⟶   _____

permission ⟶   _____

Use *ible* to keep the soft sound of *c* and *g*.

                                 Copy

el i g__ ble   * _____

le g__ ble   _____

for c__ ble   _____

tan g__ ble   _____

re du c__ ble   _____

neg li g__ ble   _____

in vin c__ ble   _____

Have another student test you on spelling the starred words. They are practical spelling words.

My score: _____ words correct.

WORKSHEET 25–G

Add *able* to the following roots. Don't forget to drop the final *e* when necessary.

			able Word		ABC Order
adore	+	able	=	_____ *	_____
comfort	+	able	=	_____ *	_____
value	+	able	=	_____ *	_____
consider	+	able	=	_____ *	_____
admire	+	able	=	_____	_____
excite	+	able	=	_____	_____
profit	+	able	=	_____ *	_____
use	+	able	=	_____	_____
compare	+	able	=	_____	_____
imagine	+	able	=	_____	_____

Add *ible* to the following roots. Drop the final *e* when necessary.

			ible Word		ABC Order
sense	+	ible	=	_____	_____
defense	+	ible	=	_____	_____
collect	+	ible	=	_____	_____
response	+	ible	=	_____ *	_____
force	+	ible	=	_____	_____
reduce	+	ible	=	_____	_____
deduct	+	ible	=	_____ *	_____

Now go back and write the words in each section in alphabetical order.

Have another student test you on spelling the starred words. They are practical spelling words.

My score: _____ words correct.

WORKSHEET 25–H

Listed below are commonly used /əbl/ words. Copy them under the correct heading, saying the sounds aloud as you spell.

possible	valuable	capable	probable	comfortable
portable	visible	adorable	eligible	profitable
suitable	variable	terrible	vegetable	responsible

able   *ible*

_____   _____   _____

_____   _____   _____

_____   _____   _____

_____   _____   _____

_____   _____   _____

Cover the top half of this worksheet. See if you can remember whether to use *able* or *ible*. Then check yourself.

valu_____   vis_____   comfort_____

ador_____   cap_____   profit_____

poss_____   prob_____   respons_____

vari_____   suit_____   veget_____

elig_____   terr_____   port_____

Find and circle the fifteen words above in the puzzle below. The words can be found in a straight line across or up and down.

```
R C O M F O R T A B L E L V E G E T A B L E
V A R I A B L E D P O S S I B L E L I G I B
A P A P O R T A B L E R E S P O N S I B L E
L A D O R A B L E L I S U I T A B L E V A L
U B O R E S P R O F I T A B L E C O M F O R
E L I G I B L E V I S V A L U A B L E B L E
T E R P R O B A B L E A T E R R I B L E L E
```

WORKSHEET 25–I

Add *able* or *ible* to make adjectives (describing words). Then cover the phrases and see if you can spell the words correctly.

a respons_____ politician   _____

a comfort_____ chair   _____

a terr_____ storm   _____

a valu_____ ring   _____

vari_____ weather   _____

a green or a yellow veget_____   _____

a profit_____ business   _____

a cap_____ physician   _____

a prob_____ event   _____

an elig_____ athlete   _____

an ador_____ baby   _____

an imposs_____ chance   _____

an invis_____ effect   _____

a suit_____ dress   _____

a port_____ television   _____

Proofing Practice: Two common List 25 words are misspelled in each of the sentences below. Correct them as shown.

               vegetables
1. If you eat your ~~vegetibles,~~ you can have a popsacle for dessert.

2. The nervous electrician did not have a plausable explanation for the stolen articals found in her garage.

3. Do you think that it is possible for a bicicle to outrun a motorcycle on the obstacal course?

4. Only an irresponsable citizen would embezzel money on the job.

5. Jack and Rachel had a terrable time trying to assembul the new portable crib.

71

WORKSHEET 25−J

-able and *-ible* are suffixes that change words into adjectives (describing words). *-able* and *-ible* mean:

>able to . . .
>
>capable of being . . .
>
>worthy of being . . .
>
>having qualities of . . .

Write the correct *able* or *ible* word from the right-hand column after each definition.

1. Easy to read (as in handwriting)	*legible*	lovable
2. Capable of being divided		avoidable
3. Capable of being removed		tangible
4. Capable of being carried		legible
5. Capable of being corrupted		collapsible
6. Capable of being defended		removable
7. Capable of being read		divisible
8. Capable of being touched		portable
9. Capable of being excited		readable
10. Capable of being collected		valuable
11. Able to collapse or fold		corruptible
12. Able to avoid		comfortable
13. Able to make a profit		excitable
14. Worthy of being loved		profitable
15. Worthy of being despised		defensible
16. Worthy of being valued		collectible
17. Having qualities of comfort		despicable

Review: *-able* and *-ible* are (accented, unaccented) endings.

When an *-able* or *-ible* word is three syllables long, the accent is always on the _____ syllable.

WORKSHEET 25-K

Match the definitions with the words listed below. Use your dictionary if necessary. Then complete the puzzle.

durable   audible   tangible   liable

navigable   invincible   educable   accessible

negligible   dispensable   visible   flexible

1. Not rigid; capable of bending   _____ (4 Down)

2. Capable of being heard   _____ (9 Across)

3. Capable of being seen   _____ (5 Down)

4. Capable of being touched   _____ (3 Down)

5. Bound by law; exposed to risk   _____ (8 Down)

6. Incapable of being conquered   _____ (11 Across)

7. Capable of lasting; not wearing out   _____ (7 Across)

8. Deep and wide enough for ships to pass through; capable of being navigated   _____ (6 Across)

9. Capable of being educated   _____ (2 Down)

10. Able to be disregarded or neglected, usually because it is so small   _____ (1 Across)

11. Easy to get to; obtainable   _____ (10 Across)

12. Able to be done without   _____ (12 Across)

WORKSHEET 25-L

Fill in each blank with a word from below that makes sense in the sentence.

miracle	invincible	deductible	flexible	negligible
audible	plausible	eligible	obstacles	considerable
liable	navigable	terrible	motorcycle	incredible

1. Geraldine is not likely to believe you even though your excuse is

   _ _ _ _ _ _ _ _.

2. The sound of the alarm was barely _ _ _ _ _ _ _. Something must be wrong with it.

3. Because of the large number of rapids and the shallowness of the river, it is not

   _ _ _ _ _ _ _ _.

4. The _ _ _ _ _ _ _ _ _ _ army fought and won in spite of all

   _ _ _ _ _ _ _ _ _.

5. Personal business expenses are _ _ _ _ _ _ _ _ _ _ items on your tax return.

6. Carlton purchased the _ _ _ _ _ _ _ _ _ _ at

   _ _ _ _ _ _ _ _ _ _ _ _ _ expense.

7. Only a _ _ _ _ _ _ _ could have saved Ms. Chester from the

   _ _ _ _ _ _ _ _ accident.

8. Although the damage was _ _ _ _ _ _ _ _ _ _, the driver of the car will

   still be _ _ _ _ _ _.

9. The _ _ _ _ _ _ _ _ gymnast will certainly be _ _ _ _ _ _ _ _ for the team.

10. It is hard to believe that we are having such warm weather in January. It is truly

    _ _ _ _ _ _ _ _ _.

Unscramble the words below and spell them correctly in the blanks. All the words can be found in the list above.

C A R M I L E   _ _ _ _ _ _ _

R I C E B I N L E D   _ _ _ _ _ _ _ _ _ _

C O I N R E A L B E D S   _ _ _ _ _ _ _ _ _ _ _

WORKSHEET 25-M

Read the following sentences and circle all the List 25 words that you can find.

1. Corn is an example of a yellow vegetable.

2. The thief was responsible for stealing the vehicles.

3. That article about soluble particles was terrible.

4. Is it possible to buy a portable radio?

5. The icicle was visible from inside the house.

6. The young child is not capable of sensible behavior.

7. This motorcycle is quite comfortable.

8. It is not probable that a miracle will occur.

9. Rosa's bicycle is valuable.

10. The adorable baby licked the cherry popsicle with visible delight.

11. You will be liable for any public funds you embezzle.

12. She is not eligible to be a disciple.

Look at List 25. Choose five words and write them in sentences below.

_____
_____
_____
_____
_____

Take out a piece of blank paper. Your teacher will dictate three of the sentences above for you to write.

You have completed the worksheets for List 25. Now it is time to check your accuracy in reading and spelling. Read and spell ten words selected by your teacher, and record your scores on the Accuracy Checklist. Work toward 90–100 percent accuracy.

When you have achieved 90–100 percent accuracy in reading, build up your reading speed. Decide on your rate goal with your teacher. Record your rate on the Proficiency Graph.

My goal for reading List 25 is _____ words per minute with two or fewer errors.

REVIEW: LISTS 20–25

lotion	*famous	flexible	*picture	inspector
*adventure	auction	*tremendous	professor	expansion
*terrible	*remember	statue	sensation	*enormous
*luggage	sensible	fluster	*expression	*frustration
situate	*language	visible	addiction	*division
*popular	gesture	*location	image	*example
*depression	*election	dictator	fixture	numerous
*position	popsicle	*physician	*measure	*occasion
*mustard	storage	motorcycle	*collision	onward
magician	punctuate	*taxation	*dangerous	*tension
tricycle	educator	*conclusion	*objection	*joyous
sausage	*admission	exposure	vinegar	*calendar
*recession	cellar	*politician	*invasion	*concentration
*literature	execution	*fabulous	solar	editor
supervision	obstacle	*confusion	auction	*future
fracture	*average	*standard	*adorable	*inspection

*Practical spelling words. The teacher and student should decide together how many of these words the student will be responsible for spelling.

SUMMARY OF ACCENT PATTERNS

Accented Syllable—An accented syllable is pronounced as if it were a one-syllable word with a clear vowel sound according to its syllabic type (*ac´ tive, com plete´, ser´ vant, loy´ al*).

Unaccented Syllable—An unaccented syllable is pronounced with a schwa /ə/ or short-*i* /ĭ/ vowel sound regardless of its syllabic type (*rib´ bon, op´ po site, in de pen´ dent*).

Accent Patterns—The dark lines and accent marks in this book are accent patterns (__´ __). Each line stands for one syllable. The accent mark shows which syllable is accented. Learning to place the accent on the proper syllable will help you recognize most multisyllabic words. The accent patterns below will help you determine which syllable in a word is accented.

Primary Accent—A strong stress on a syllable in a multisyllabic word.

Secondary Accent—A weaker stress on a syllable in a multisyllabic word.

General Guideline—In two- and three-syllable words, accent the first syllable. Then pronounce the first vowel as if it were a short, long, *r*-controlled, or double-vowel sound in a one-syllable word. If that doesn't make a recognizable word, accent the second syllable, and pronounce the second vowel according to its syllabic type.

Accent Patterns for Two-Syllable Words

1. Accent on the first syllable (__´ __)
   The accent is usually on the first syllable in two-syllable words (*stan´ dard, sis´ ter, dol´ lar*).

2. Accent on the second syllable (__ __´)
   Two-syllable words that have a prefix in the first syllable and a root in the second syllable are usually accented on the second syllable (*ex tend´, con fuse´*).

3. Accent on either the first or second syllable (__´ __ or __ __´)
   If a word can function as both noun and verb, the noun is accented on the prefix (*con´ duct*) and the verb is accented on the root (*con duct´*).

Accent Patterns for Three-Syllable Words

1. Accent on the first syllable (__´ __ __)
   The accent is usually on the first syllable in three-syllable words. The unaccented middle syllable has a schwa sound (*vis´ i tor, char´ ac ter*).

2. Accent on the second syllable (__ __´ __)
   The accent is usually on the second syllable (the root) in words that contain a prefix, root, and suffix (*de stroy´ er, in ven´ tor*).

Accent Patterns for Four-Syllable Words (__ __´ __ __)

1. The accent is usually on the second syllable in four-syllable words (*in tel´ li gence, sig nif´ i cant*).

Special Accent Patterns for Words of Three or More Syllables

Accent patterns for words longer than two syllables are often governed by a specific ending pattern or an unaccented vowel.

1. Accent with the ending *-ic*
   Accent the syllable just before the ending *-ic* (*fran´ tic, e las´ tic, en er get´ ic, char ac ter is´ tic*).

2. Accent with the ending *-ate* /āt/
   In three-syllable words, the first syllable has a primary accent and *-ate* has a secondary accent (*vi´ o late´*).
   In four-syllable words, the second syllable has a primary accent and *-ate* has a secondary accent (*con grat´ u late´*).

3. Accent with schwa endings
   Schwa endings (and schwa syllables) are never accented. The accent falls on another syllable in the word (*pleas´ ant, in´ no cent, ex ter´ nal, ap pren´ tice*).

4. Accent with the endings *-tion, -sion, -cian*
   Accent the syllable just before the endings *-tion, -sion,* and *-cian* (*pol lu´ tion, im pres´ sion, ad min is tra´ tion, e lec tri´ cian*).

5. Accent with the ending *-ity* /ĭ tē/.
   Accent the syllable just before the ending *-ity* (*qual´ i ty, ac tiv´ i ty, per son al´ i ty*).

6. Accent in words with an unaccented middle syllable
   Accent the syllable just before the unaccented middle syllable with *i* as /ə/, *i* as /ē/, and *u* as /ə/ or /ū/ (*sim´ i lar, aud´ i ence, par tic´ u lar*).

7. *Accent in words with i as /y/*
   Accent the syllable just before the unaccented syllable with *i* as /y/ (*com pan´ ion, in con ven´ ient, mem or a bil´ ia*).

8. Accent in words with *ti* or *ci* as /sh/
   Accent the syllable just before a final syllable with *ti* or *ci* as /sh/ (*fi nan´ cial, pres i den´ tial*).

ACCURACY CHECKLIST
Megawords 4, Lists 20–25

Student _____

Record accuracy score as a fraction: $\dfrac{\text{\# correct}}{\text{\# attempted}}$

List	Examples	Check Test Scores Date:		Reading			Spelling		
		Reading	Spelling						
20. *-er, -or, -ar, -ard, -ward*	elevator blizzard								
21. *-tion*	portion solution								
22. *-sion, -cian*	vision optician								
23. *-ous, -age*	fabulous advantage								
24. *-ture, -tu-, -sure*	departure punctuate composure								
25. *-able, -ible,* Consonant-*le*	probable divisible vehicle								
Review: Lists 20–25									

PROFICIENCY GRAPH

Student_____

Goal_____

●———● Words Read Correctly

×———× Errors

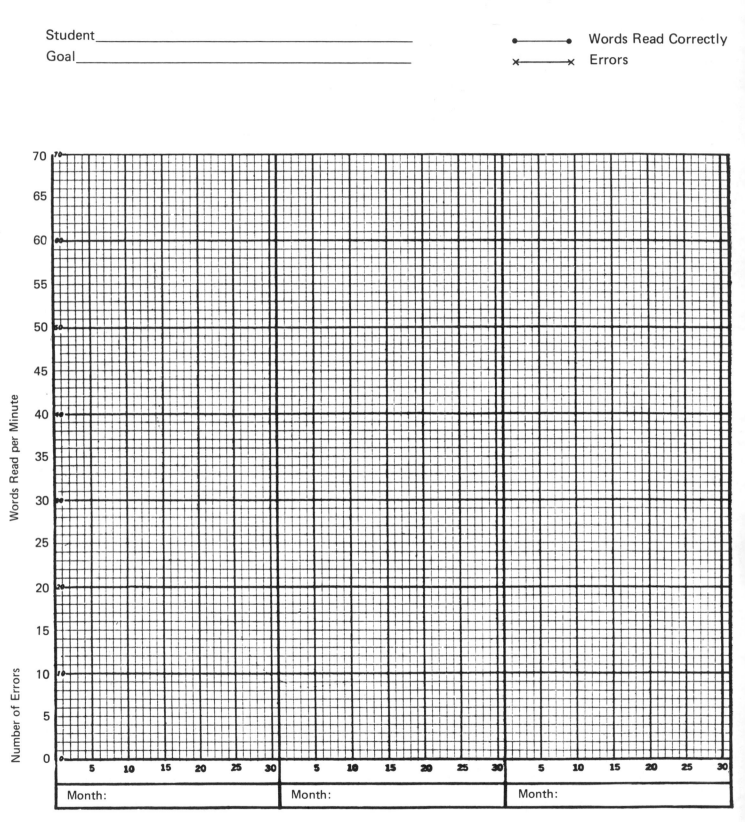

Words Read per Minute

Number of Errors

Month:

Month:

Month:

Calendar Days

PROFICIENCY GRAPH

Student_____

Goal_____

●———● Words Read Correctly

✕———✕ Errors

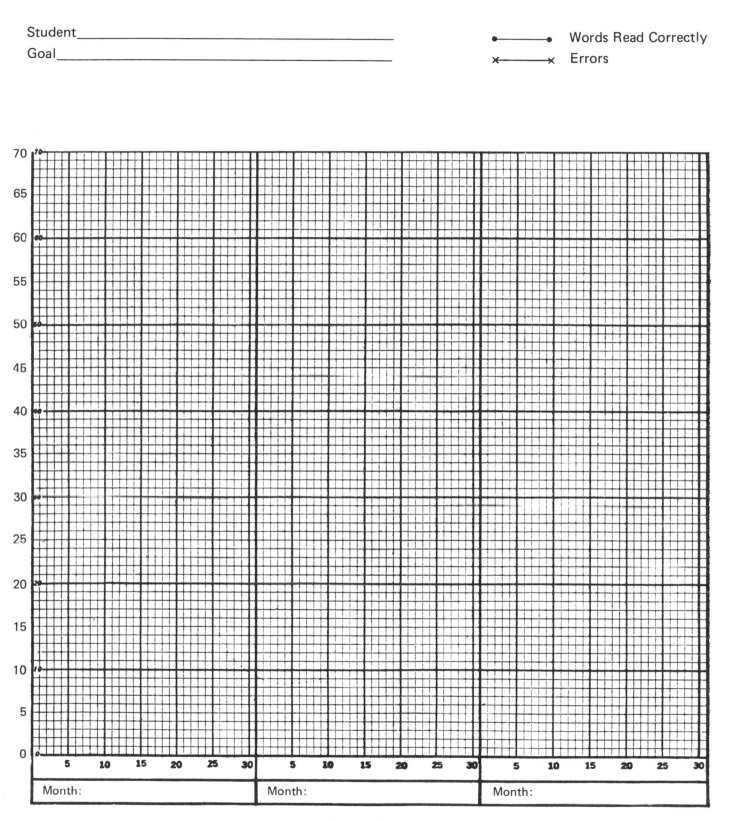

Calendar Days

81

PROFICIENCY GRAPH

Student_____

Goal_____

●———————● Words Read Correctly

✕———————✕ Errors

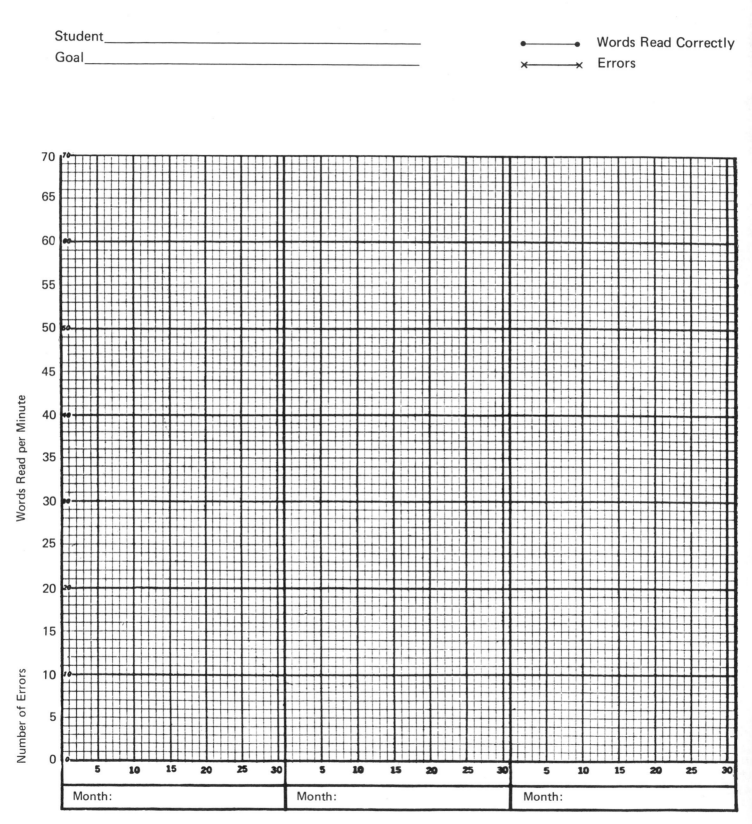

Words Read per Minute

Number of Errors

Calendar Days

EXAMINER'S RECORDING FORM—READING

Check Test: Lists 20–25
Megawords 4

Name _____   Date _____

20. -er, -or, -ar, -ard, and -ward

destroyer
calculator
circular
custard
afterward

correct _____

21. -tion

junction
cognition
solution
consultation
administration

correct _____

22. -sion and -cian

confession
percussion
musician
diversion
mathematician

correct _____

23. -ous and -age

sausage
voyage
monstrous
savage
prosperous

correct _____

24. -ture, -tu-, and -sure

curvature
actual
exposure
pasture
congratulate

correct _____

25. -able, -ible, and Consonant-le

applicable
audible
vehicle
flexible
imaginable

correct _____

Total Correct _____

Total Possible ___30___

Name _____   Date _____

20. -er, -or, -ar, -ard, and -ward

destroyer
calculator
circular
custard
afterward

\# correct _____

21. -tion

junction
cognition
solution
consultation
administration

\# correct _____

22. -sion and -cian

confession
percussion
musician
diversion
mathematician

\# correct _____

23. -ous and -age

sausage
voyage
monstrous
savage
prosperous

\# correct _____

24. -ture, -tu-, and -sure

curvature
actual
exposure
pasture
congratulate

\# correct _____

25. -able, -ible, and Consonant-le

applicable
audible
vehicle
flexible
imaginable

\# correct _____

Total Correct _____
Total Possible ___30___

84